MAZE

Solve the World's Most Challenging Puzzle

by Christopher Manson

An Owl Book HENRY HOLT AND COMPANY/NEW YORK

Distributed by MindWare, Roseville MN 1-800-999-0398

To my family. . . .   C.M.

Henry Holt and Company, LLC
Publishers since 1866
115 West 18th Street
New York, New York 10011

Henry Holt® is a registered trademark
of Henry Holt and Company, LLC.

Library of Congress Cataloging-in-Publication Data
Manson, Christopher.
Maze.
ISBN 0-8050-1088-2 (An Owl Book: pbk.)
1. Literary recreations.   2. Riddles.
I. Title.
GV1493.M26   1985   793.73   85-8619

Henry Holt books are available for special promotions
and premiums. For details contact: Director, Special Markets.

Designed by Amy Hill

Printed in the United States of America

15

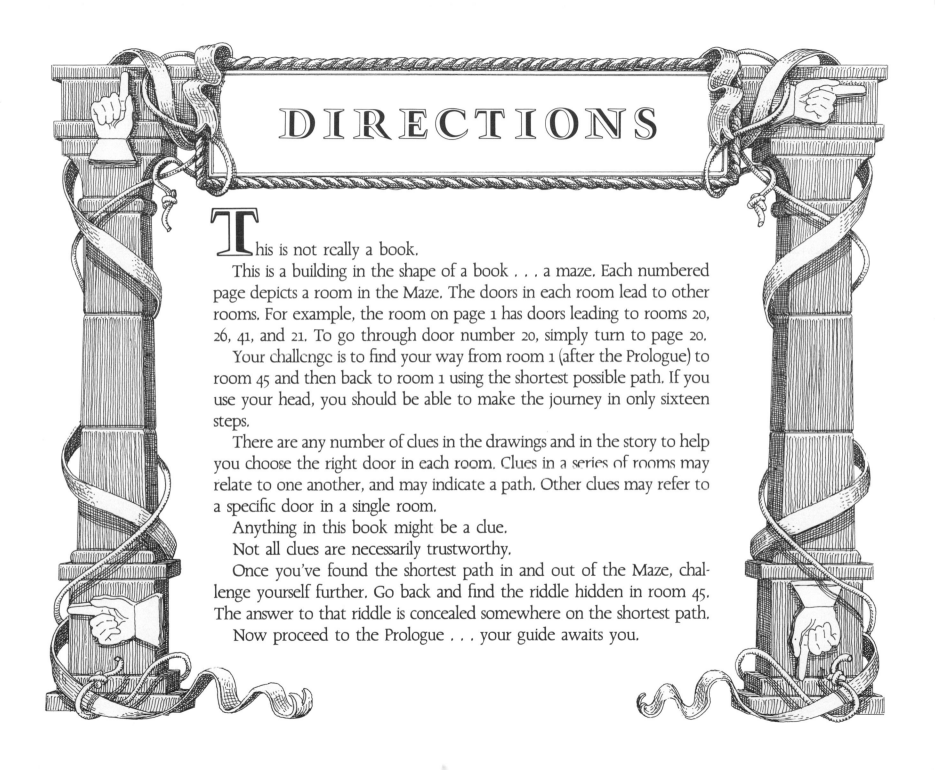

DIRECTIONS

This is not really a book.

This is a building in the shape of a book . . . a maze. Each numbered page depicts a room in the Maze. The doors in each room lead to other rooms. For example, the room on page 1 has doors leading to rooms 20, 26, 41, and 21. To go through door number 20, simply turn to page 20.

Your challenge is to find your way from room 1 (after the Prologue) to room 45 and then back to room 1 using the shortest possible path. If you use your head, you should be able to make the journey in only sixteen steps.

There are any number of clues in the drawings and in the story to help you choose the right door in each room. Clues in a series of rooms may relate to one another, and may indicate a path. Other clues may refer to a specific door in a single room.

Anything in this book might be a clue.

Not all clues are necessarily trustworthy.

Once you've found the shortest path in and out of the Maze, challenge yourself further. Go back and find the riddle hidden in room 45. The answer to that riddle is concealed somewhere on the shortest path.

Now proceed to the Prologue . . . your guide awaits you.

PROLOGUE

The Maze.

I met them at the gate though I usually wait inside. Preoccupied with their own thoughts, impatient, like so many children, they didn't see who I really was. They never noticed my crown, my pain, the fire in my eyes.

Like all the others they think the Maze was made for them; actually, it is the other way around. They think I am some poet who will lead them through the symbols and spaces of this Underworld. They think I will teach them lessons. They should call me Cerberus. . . . I am the lesson.

The monstrous walls rise up and run away as far as the human eye can see, circling and dividing. Which half is the Maze?

Even I get lost. It changes—sometimes slowly, imperceptibly . . . sometimes suddenly. This House is not only made of stone and mortar, wood and paint; it is made of time and mystery, hope and fear. Construction never stops. I take some pride in my role as architect.

They think I will guide them to the center. Perhaps I will. . . .

The sun was very hot.

Together we walked through the gate into . . .

. . . the entrance hall of the Maze.

They looked carefully at the bronze doors, trying to choose. The uncertainty of visitors is one of my little pleasures.

"It's easy to get lost," I said helpfully. "This can be a sinister place." The sun glared at me through the gateway.

Something was ringing behind one of the doors. They spent some time trying to decide which door it was, not understanding that the silences of the Maze are as eloquent as the sounds.

"Decisions, decisions," one said. "Too many decisions."

"The story of my life," said another.

"We don't want to be late," said a third, opening one of the doors.

"Nary a soul to be seen," said the first, peering into the gloom.

I waited patiently for them to choose which way to go . . . into . . .

. . . a bright room whose walls were in some disrepair. The floorboards creaked and groaned; the plaster made a gritty sound.

They studied the old frescoes for clues but missed the obvious signs.

"Are we on the right path?" they asked.

Keeping in mind what a relative term "right" is, I assured them they were, indeed, on the right path. As for the "correct" path or the "most appropriate" path. . . . Well, that might be something else.

Full of confidence now they marched out to . . .

. . . an entirely different kind of place.

The group complained of feeling "all turned around," as well they might.

Because no one wanted to stay here very long they missed the real sign while looking through the obvious. People in their situation, confronted with a challenge, tend to accept the terms of the challenge as a given, without examining it from all sides. How many sides does that problem have? They don't know.

We passed down a long flight of stairs, through some sort of pantry, and on into . . .

. . . the great hall of many doors.

"What a foolish face," I snorted. "Pay no attention."

A sound made them all turn suddenly. A small black cat ran out of a door to my right, sniffed at us, and, before I could move, ran out of the hall. It was fortunate that I was still standing with the rest of them or they might have noticed.

Faint voices came down one of the corridors.

"Shall we toss a coin?" I asked. "Or have you made up your minds?"

They hadn't made up their minds, and they had no coins. By a process of elimination they decided to go to . . .

. . . the tree room.

"Are these real?" they asked.

I told them the trees were as real as anything else in the House. As this was an important decision I encouraged them to take their time. After all, the more they think about the possibilities the more choices they have to make.

What were their chances of choosing wisely . . . one in four? Two in four perhaps, if I was generous about it . . . and why not be generous? There are one hundred ninety doors in this part of the House, counting the gate . . . enough for everyone.

Making a choice, they entered a very long, dark corridor and at last came out into . . .

forthwith
forthright
forthward
forth ___

43   22   30   20

5

. . . a gloomy, cavelike place far underground. Even I was oppressed by the weight that hung over our heads. A very small hole, high above, admitted a feeble light.

Standing in the light one of them put his hand out. "I think it may be raining out there . . ."

They didn't like the look of the place.

"You continue to judge everything by the way it looks!" I cried, exasperated by their timidity. I knew I shouldn't have said anything. If you think of all the deceptions practiced in my family, particularly on my father . . .

We went down the only way open to us and came to . . .

. . . a pleasant room with three doors and a lamp. Looking at the picture on the wall they decided it wasn't a very good likeness.

One of them almost fell over something on the floor. "Why don't they pick up after themselves?" he said, sounding like an old man.

"Weren't you ever irresponsible?" I asked, thinking of my childhood and how wild I had been.

Music was being played somewhere nearby. We stopped to listen for a moment.

Leaving the pictures looking out at an empty room we went on to . . .

. . . a vaulted chamber lit by a single bulb.

Someone knocked a bowl off the table. The crash echoed from the ceiling and whispered away down the corridors. I broke another on purpose.

"Make sure to take that with you," I said. "You can never tell when you might need it."

"Take what?" they wanted to know.

"Isn't it obvious?"

Taking a vote among themselves they went on to . . .

. . . what appeared to be an old storeroom. Dust obscured a damaged painting making it hard to understand just what the artist had intended.

"This could be a trick of some sort," one said. "We might be going around in circles."

"I don't think so," said the thoughtful one, "I think we're supposed to think it's a trick . . . that's the trick."

They all looked at me. "Yes," I said. "I'm sure you're right about that."

With doubtful looks they left for . . .

. . . a room that smelled of paint. Faint voices, apparently in an argument, came from behind the locked door.

"You know," said one, "that sounds like us in there . . ."

They tried the door but, naturally, it wouldn't open. The voices stopped when the doorknob rattled.

One picked up the umbrella. "It may rain where we're going."

I signaled my approval and, after a short rest, we came to . . .

. . . an airy room with many doors. It was a big space, but I still felt crowded. I've always hated confinement.

"Whatever you do," I warned them, "don't touch that!"

"This must be an important room," said one of them. "It has more doors than any of the others . . ."

This was not true but I didn't want to interrupt.

"With so many paths crossing here we must be close to the center," she continued.

I had noticed this guest before; I would have to be careful. "This is an important choice," I said, trying to encourage them.

Gratefully leaving the room behind we walked all the way to . . .

. . . a spacious room with a hole in the floor. A ladder led down into the shadows. Outside, leaves shook in the wind. They didn't like the look of that hole in the floor.

"Too dark down there!" they cried. "Who knows what's at the bottom." They looked at me again.

"Probably a room of some kind," I volunteered quickly. "But you know what I say about appearances." It would have been a relief to get outside for a while.

They wanted to know if they had been here before. . . . How could I answer that?

"I have the strangest feeling of déjà vu," said one who, bolder than the rest, led us into . . .

. . . room number 13.

They weren't really comfortable here and I knew why.

"No, no," they said. "We're not all superstitious."

"Only some of you, then?"

They were worried it might be Friday. Well, it's true that it was closer to the end of the week than they realized. It takes a great deal of experience, certainly more than they possessed, to understand how time works in the Maze. The clock thought it was six in the evening.

Quickly moving on we came to . . .

. . . one of the biggest rooms in the House. All three doorways were dark.

"Afraid to go out?" I asked.

Since they tried to think of themselves as adults, they didn't care for my question.

"Not really," said the thoughtful one, "but that doesn't mean we have to go running around out there just to prove something to you."

I knew she would bear watching.

"Choose then!" I cried, as if my feelings were hurt. "Pay no attention to anything I say." I knew they couldn't afford not to listen to me entirely . . . they were so easily led.

Turning around, the group took a path that completely surprised me after all, and I followed them to . . .

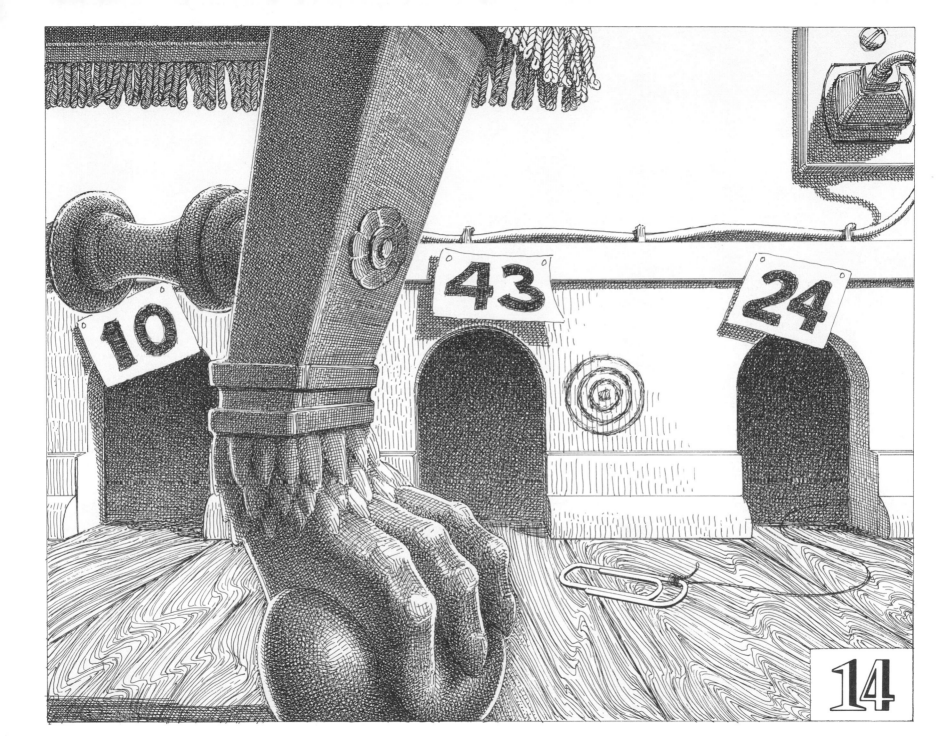

. . . room number 15. Just as we entered I heard a thump and the sound of footsteps hurrying away. Somewhere a door slammed.

"At least three of us can sit down here," said one.

There were only three possible choices.

Leaning on the sacrificial tripod I was suddenly moved to say, "Perhaps these numbers relate to each other in some specific combination . . ." Immediately I regretted this act of charity . . . sometimes I think, after all these years, that I don't really know myself.

One of them thought he had worked it out and, very pleased with himself, led us into . . .

. . . a stone chamber which reminded me of my old neighbors. Of course, that was a long time ago now, but would you believe their descendants are still telling stories about me and my family to their children?

Even if most of the stories are lies and exaggerations, it is immortality of a sort.

As I passed in front of an open doorway a figure, crossing the hall outside, saw me and immediately ran off.

"Who was that?" they asked.

"Another visitor, to be sure."

"Why did he run away?"

"You probably scared him," I said, and they apparently believed me.

With few regrets on my part we left for . . .

. . . a room with a floor of sand.

"Amphorae," I pronounced; empty, of course.

"This is an easier choice to make," they said.

"You may think so," I muttered to myself, "but your choices are more limited than you know."

One should never accept the obvious here. If you think of the Maze as a machine, confusion is its product, and the machine was hard at work.

Ignoring my good advice they hurried into . . .

. . . a much warmer room. Shadows danced across the floor to the fire's music.

"Someone's lost his hat."

"Are you sure it's the hat that is lost?" I asked reasonably enough. No one would answer me.

Ducking behind a curtain and hurrying down a passageway we came out in . . .

. . . a shaded portico. A late afternoon sun warmed the rough blocks of stone.

"Get out of the way!" someone called. We moved into the yard, squinting at the strong light.

One of them sat on a marble bench after I politely pushed some flowers aside. "Did you pick these for me?" she asked, looking me in the eye. I had to tell her the truth.

In another part of the grounds someone was singing but they couldn't make out the words.

Like children they soon became restless and impatient to see something new, so we went on to . . .

. . . room number 20. The ringing stopped as soon as we entered.

"What is the matter now?" I asked them.

"Too many animals for a proper house!"

They walked carefully around the edges of the room. I watched with an amusement shared, I think, by the wise old tortoise.

With backward looks and muttered comments about turtles they left room number 20 and entered . . .

20

. . . a yard containing shrubs trimmed in ornamental shapes.

"This," I began, "is called . . ."

"We know what the name is," they interrupted. "Why don't you just tell us which way to go?"

"I wasn't referring to the plants," I said in a huff. I refused to say anything else, leaving them to find their own way to . . .

. . . a gaudy room that reminded me of a theatrical backdrop. Places like this are overdone, for my taste, but some people like the exotic . . . well, everyone is a critic.

It's true, I am by nature extremely critical. Although my life is a lonely one I have not spared any of my guests the rigor of my judgment. . . . We all have our roles to play.

This is not a bad place, really; one could spend quite some time here. However, in their restive way, the group moved on to . . .

. . . a room with three other doors. Looking out the windows my feet crushed something on the floor.

"Watch your step here," I warned them. I'm always ready to be helpful with the less important things.

"Look at those two trees out there," one said, looking over my shoulder, which is not easy to do.

"Must be a real wind coming up."

Now they realized that it could rain where they were going.

"We should have brought that bumbershoot with us from the coat room . . ."

"Which room was that?"

"You remember, the one with the animal . . ."

I suggested that we take the door on my right and they realized they had found the door they had been seeking for so long, the entrance to . . .

. . . a place of unlimited darkness.

"Where are the doors?" they asked nervously. "We can't see any doors . . ."

"Be careful where you step!" said a cold voice. "This spot is taken." Dozens of eyes blinked at us in the Stygian gloom.

By the time my uncertain visitors turned to ask me what to do I was already far away.

"There are no doors," said the voice. "You are here with the rest of us now . . ."

Even my bellowing laughter couldn't fill this space.

24

. . . a high room with the image of a crown on the wall for everyone to see now. Though one of my parents might be lowborn, the other was close to a king. . . . I've always felt at home here.

"Which door ought we take?" they wanted to know. I rather brusquely indicated the three doors.

"Any of these is fine for my purposes."

They were disconcerted at the apparent lack of clues. "Perhaps in another room," they said, leaving for . . .

. . . a dramatic room with four entrances and exits.

"Not enough light in here," they remarked. "Not very tidy either."

"Which way now, children?" I asked in my most patronizing voice.

They objected to my tone, but it distracted them from the real clues. The game usually goes as I plan it, despite the intentions of my visitors, or perhaps because of their intentions.

"What the devil is this supposed to be?" one asked. They gathered around and I realized they were close to something. I quickly picked up the bell, ringing it loudly.

"Was this what you heard outside?"

Holding their ears they ran out the door to . . .

. . . a darkened chamber dominated by a large figure.

We could see that someone had been working here recently; the entrance I had so carefully hidden had been uncovered. I made a note to return as soon as I could and fill in the hole again.

The visitors were so intrigued with the entrance at the bottom of the excavation that they ignored what the figure was trying to tell them

"Where are the workmen?"

"They must be ahead of us," I said. "If we hurry we can catch them . . . I mean catch up with them."

I herded the group through the door to . . .

. . . a spacious room with a hole in the floor. A ladder led down into the shadows. Outside, leaves shook in the wind. They didn't like the look of that hole in the floor.

"Too dark down there!" they cried. "Who knows what's at the bottom." They looked at me again.

"Probably a room of some kind," I volunteered quickly. "But you know what I say about appearances." It would have been a relief to get outside for a while.

They wanted to know if they had been here before. . . . How could I answer that?

"I have the strangest feeling of déjà vu," said one who, bolder than the rest, led us into . . .

. . . a much smaller room.

A person with a white staff turned to face us. His associate shrugged, not an easy thing to do in his position, and went back to what he had been doing.

"Look, look," said the person with the staff. "This is very important . . ."

I snatched the paper from his hand and tore it to pieces.

"How will he find his way without directions?" the group wanted to know.

"Don't worry," said the man, "here blindness is no disadvantage."

I hurried my visitors out as quickly as I could to . . .

. . . room number 30. "What a beautiful door . . . the others are so plain," said one.

"It's meant to influence our decision," said another.

"Perhaps this has been done so we will not choose this door," said the thoughtful one.

They wanted to know what the letters meant. Obviously they meant something, and I said so.

"Yes, but . . . why 'O' and 'U'? What special significance can they have for us?"

The more confused they became, the more I enjoyed it. No matter how many times I've been through this I'm always fascinated.

Leaving the room and all that it contained behind us, we entered . . .

. . . a melancholy little courtyard surrounded by a brick wall too high to see over. A dead tree lifted its bone-white branches to a sky filling with gray clouds.

"Those doors look very strange," they said.

"You should say, 'They look very strangely,' " I corrected.

"They seem to be watching us . . ."

A sudden gust of wind made the branches clatter against each other like old boards. Dead leaves began to gather at our feet.

Shivering in the wind we managed to push open one of the heavy doors and make our way to . . .

. . . a large square room with a hole rudely broken through one wall. It must have taken a great deal of strength to pull the heavy stones out of position.

The symmetry was also disturbed by the apparent loss of one of the room's statues. My visitors thought a thief had broken into the room, removed the figure, and made away with it. This, of course, was one explanation.

"Another one!" they cried.

"You mean another representative of the animal kingdom?" I asked.

"What is a bird like that doing here?"

"Roosting, evidently." Their attitude was really beginning to irritate me. I have come to think of all the inhabitants of this House as members of my little kingdom. People can be so arrogant . . . in a very real way we are all of us animals, at least in part.

I wouldn't answer any more of their questions so we left this room to enter . . .

. . . the room with no floor. They crowded each other on the narrow ledge. The bold one ventured out to the center.

Realizing that they could see all of the signs only from the center of the room, several wanted to turn back.

With exaggerated caution, considering their predicament, they finally reached the door they wanted and eventually found themselves in . . .

. . . a middle-class drawing room or parlor. It was amazing how much more comfortable they felt in these surroundings.

Everyone sat down, some on the floor, and chatted about where they had been and where they should go.

"Magpies!" I said to myself. "Not a real thought in their heads."

They were so much at ease they almost missed what the room was telling them altogether. They finally got the message, which I thought was pretty obvious, and we went on to . . .

. . . what appeared to be someone's basement. One of them sank gratefully down on an old couch which promptly collapsed.

I tried to hide my smile.

"A totem, or tribal fetish," said one, walking around the center of the room.

"It could be a work of art," suggested another.

"Perhaps it's a signal to us," the thoughtful one said. "A warning or direction?"

"Not much help when there is only one way to go," put in another.

"I still think it's a signal."

"Yes," I said right away, "I'm sure you're right."

She was immediately suspicious. Still, with no real choice to make, we left the thing standing alone in light and silence, and went into . . .

. . . an old and ruinous part of the House. Turning a corner the music we had been hearing became louder and at last we saw the musicians themselves.

They were so involved they failed to hear us. The music was suited to the scene—a moody, romantic melody. We stopped to listen and I admit that I, too, was affected by the sound as well as by the spectacle of the masked players.

One of the visitors noticed me listening. "Beautiful music, don't you think?"

"It's not bad," I said stiffly. "The viol brings the right sense of warmth to the piece, but the guitarist is overplaying his part. Still, he adds a certain plangent brio to an otherwise introspective composition . . ."

Unwilling to interrupt the concert we slipped past the musicians into the door to . . .

. . . a long, open room with no roof.

"What is going on here?" they wondered.

"Sometimes, important messages are couched in ambiguous terms," I said. "That net may help you catch the answer to your question."

They looked doubtful. "We must look at this from all sides before we make a decision." At last, they were learning.

They really couldn't decide which way to go; half of them wanted to go one way, half another. They were close to splitting up when there was a rattling sound and one of the doors was shaken from the other side.

They all stopped talking and moved closer together. They soon agreed on a direction and we departed for . . .

. . . a narrow space where one wall boasted half-finished carvings and another some sort of carnival poster. There was a little confusion as we made our entrance but we soon sorted ourselves out.

It was impossible to climb up the slippery slide and another door wouldn't open for us, so after emptying the pebbles from our shoes, we marched on to . . .

. . . what looked like a combination wine cellar and junk room. Someone had been working here as well.

"This is more to my taste," said one, dusting off some labels. All the bottles turned out to be empty.

"I hear someone hammering," said one.

"No, that's a chopping sound," said another.

None of them heard the faint jingling that came from behind the wall. "I don't hear anything," I said loudly and, with as much commotion as possible, hurried them out of the room to . . .

. . . the foundation of the Maze. Deep underground stones had been carved and fitted; passages opened in the natural rock.

"These symbols are quite unusual," said one. "They seem to be primitive signs . . ."

"Do you know what signs?" I asked him.

"Oh, you know . . . wind and water, hills and planets."

It was surprising that he could identify any of the symbols, but I was relieved that he couldn't read them correctly.

Choosing more or less at random they went through a passageway to . . .

. . . a room with a special piece of furniture I thought might appeal to my guests.

"How can we trust that thing?" one remarked. "Who knows where it ends up . . ."

I knew, naturally, but that wasn't the point. They were pretty sure of themselves, and went right on to . . .

. . . the next room.

In one corner a savage animal appeared ready to leap out, roaring, rending with tusk and claw . . . but it was only a bit of taxidermy after all.

I suggested they might wish to hang up their coats before going on.

"How will we find them?" one asked. "We might not pass through here again."

I assured them I would help them to return. "You can count on me," I said sincerely. Still, they wouldn't leave anything behind.

Opening one of the doors we made our way to . . .

. . . a great hall, dominated by the entrance to room 22. The face over the door had a sly look.

"Is it good or bad to have only two choices?" they wanted to know.

It was, predictably enough, neither "good" nor "bad." These people just didn't know how to phrase a meaningful question. You have to be very particular in this House.

We went on to . . .

. . . a courtyard of palms and statues. The trees waved to each other in the breeze.

"Who left the door open?" they wanted to know.

"We came in that way," I offered, but they were convinced we had entered by another door entirely.

They vanished through the wall and I followed them to . . .

. . . the room at the center of the Maze.

My guests thought that whoever lived here was a careless person, to leave so many things around. They were wrong.

There was really only one thing for them to find: the Riddle of the Maze. They demanded that I show it to them.

"Do you think it is written on the wall for all to see? It is hidden here, somewhere, perhaps throughout the room. As far as you are concerned, what the Maze teaches can be learned in every room."

They looked and looked . . . every group is the same.

"Now," I said, after a last look around, "we must find our way back out."

Leaving the center of the Maze we found ourselves in . . .